Basho's
Haiku Journeys

TEXT BY

Freeman Ng

ILLUSTRATIONS BY

Cassandra Rockwood Ghanem

Stone Bridge Press • Berkeley, California

Published by
Stone Bridge Press
P. O. Box 8208, Berkeley, CA 94707
TEL 510-524-8732 • sbp@stonebridge.com • www.stonebridge.com

p-ISBN 978-1-61172-069-3
e-ISBN 978-1-61172-951-1

For more about this book and haiku activities for kids, go to Freeman Ng's website www.bashopb.com/.

For more about Cassandra Rockwood Ghanem and her work, go to www.cassandrarockwoodghanem.com or Instagram @ cassandrarockwoodghanem.

Matsuo Basho was a Japanese poet who was born in 1644. He had great success writing and teaching in the big capital city of Edo (today's Tokyo), but he was never satisfied with his life there. After a fire burned down his hut, he decided to adopt a wayfaring, or traveling, life. From 1684 to 1689, he made five great journeys and wrote about them in books that have become some of the most well-known works of Japanese literature. . . .

Who was that poet
who walked the fine city streets
but without a smile?

Basho the teacher,
gazing from blossomed gardens
to the wilds beyond.

His students built him
a hut outside the city.
Then, one night, a fire!

The poet, bereft
of all but his words, wandered
deep into the woods.

The oddest feeling
swirled around him like the wind.
Was it happiness?

"Forever afoot,"
thought Basho, "seeking the Way:
I could live like this."

Basho's First Journey

Autumn 1684 – Summer 1685

In his life's Autumn,
Basho made his first journey,
packing no supplies.

Bleached bones on the road.
"What creature found its rest here?
How far had it come?"

A rose of Sharon
that blooms for only one day
of its short, sweet Spring.

In all its glory
at one moment. In the next,

devoured by his horse!

Basho's Second Journey
October 1687

The Kashima moon:
How Basho longed to see it
in Autumn fullness.

With him on the quest,
a monk and a samurai,
two unlikely friends.

Reaching the mountains:
the friends – and clouds. On the night
of the full moon: rain!

The samurai stormed.
The monk lamented. Basho,
eyes closed, only smiled.

More beautiful still
was the moon that was not there,

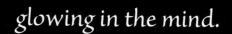

glowing in the mind.

Basho's Third Journey

November 1687 – May 1688

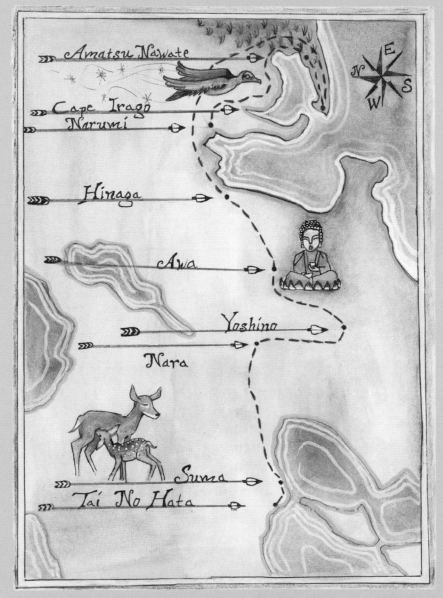

"I have traveled West,"
thought Basho, "but did not see
everything I could."

A hut standing plain
upon a desolate moor
for no eyes to see.

On Buddha's birthday,
caught between strength and weakness:
a newborn spirit.

Basho's Fourth Journey

Autumn 1688

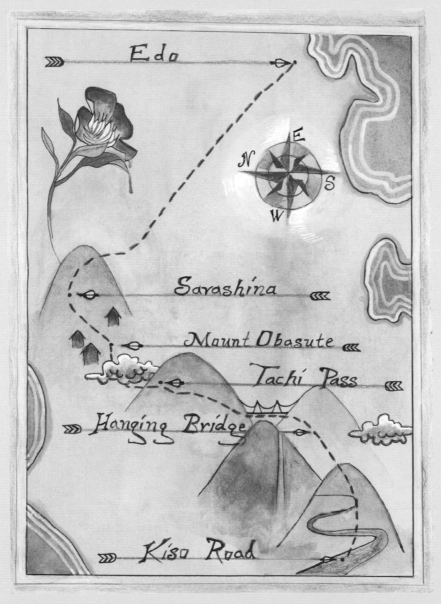

Drawn by Autumn swirls,
up Kiso Road, winding like
a path to the sky.

Mountains above him
in layers like clouds. Below,
a thousand-foot fall.

Perched on the luggage
atop a high horse, dizzy
from height above height.

"How Buddha must gaze,
with compassion from afar,
on our shaky steps."

Basho's Fifth Journey

May – October 1689

West and East and South.
What road remained untraveled?
The uttermost North.

The Sunshine Temple,
built a thousand years before,
still casting its light.

An oceanside inn.
Opening wide his window
to sleep on the sky.

A sudden illness.
A poet preparing for
his final journey.

Basho Wayfarer
travels on in the spirit,
like silk on the wind.

"Nothing does not glow
like the Moon, nothing does not
flower in that light."

"Within these old bones,
torn easily by the wind,
there is a something."

"The months and the days:
they themselves are Wayfarers,
the Way itself Home."

Basho's Haiku

Basho is most famous for writing haiku, very short poems that follow certain rules about each line. In English today, people often write haiku with five syllables in the first line, seven in the second, and five again in the third and final line, though that's not the only way to do it, and many haiku poets follow additional rules about what should be talked about in the poem.

This book was written in haiku that follow the 5-7-5 pattern, so you can see how the syllable counting works by looking at any stanza, like the very first one:

1   2   3   4 5
Who was that poet

1   2   3   4   5 6   7
who walked the fine city streets

1   2   3   4   5
but without a smile?

Basho's most famous haiku went like this:

Silent ancient pond:
the frog makes a sudden leap.
Splash! goes the water.

It might not seem like much, but that's the beauty of haiku. They can be about the simplest things. A single sight or simple thought. In just three lines. Basho himself said that writing haiku was easy. You could try writing one yourself!